AFGHANISTAN: HUMAN RIGHTS

EXECUTIVE SUMMARY

Afghanistan is an Islamic republic with a strong, directly elected presidency, a bicameral legislative branch, and a judicial branch. President Hamid Karzai was elected to a second term in 2009, and parliamentary elections were last held in 2010. There were reports of widespread fraud and irregularities in both. Civilian authorities generally maintained control over the security forces, although there were instances in which security forces acted independently and sometimes committed human rights abuses.

The most significant human rights problems were torture and abuse of detainees; increased targeted violence and endemic societal discrimination against women and girls; widespread violence, including armed insurgent groups' killings of persons affiliated with the government and indiscriminate attacks on civilians; and pervasive official corruption.

Other human rights problems included extrajudicial killings by security forces; poor prison conditions; ineffective government investigations of abuses and torture by local security forces; arbitrary arrest and detention, including of women accused of so-called moral crimes; prolonged pretrial detention; judicial corruption and ineffectiveness; violations of privacy rights; restrictions on freedom of speech and press; restrictions on freedom of religion; limits on freedom of movement; underage and forced marriages; abuse of children, including sexual abuse; discrimination and abuses against ethnic minorities; trafficking in persons; discrimination against persons with disabilities; societal discrimination based on race, religion, gender, sexual orientation, and HIV/AIDS status; abuse of worker rights; and sex and labor trafficking.

Widespread disregard for the rule of law and official impunity for those who committed human rights abuses were serious problems. The government did not prosecute abuses by officials consistently or effectively.

The Taliban and other insurgents continued to kill civilians and security force personnel using improvised explosive devices, car bombs, and suicide attacks. The Taliban used children as suicide bombers. Antigovernment elements also threatened, robbed, and attacked villagers, foreigners, civil servants, and medical and nongovernmental organization (NGO) workers.

Section 1. Respect for the Integrity of the Person, Including Freedom from:

a. Arbitrary or Unlawful Deprivation of Life

There were several credible reports that the government or its agents committed arbitrary or unlawful killings. For example, the UN Assistance Mission in Afghanistan (UNAMA) reported that in January an Afghan Local Police (ALP) commander and several ALP members broke into a home in the Chardara District of Kunduz Province and killed a 65-year-old man and two women before stealing valuables from the home and fleeing.

NGOs, UNAMA, and media reports continued to allege that Kandahar provincial chief of police Abdul Raziq facilitated extrajudicial killings.

There were numerous reports of politically motivated killings, overwhelmingly by the Taliban and other insurgent groups. The midyear UNAMA report attributed 74 percent of all civilian casualties in the first half of the year (1,038 civilian deaths and 1,825 civilian injuries) to antigovernment elements and found a 29 percent increase in civilian casualties (including deaths and injuries) resulting from targeted killings, compared with the same period in 2012. Nine percent of civilian casualties were attributed to progovernment forces during the same time period and mostly resulted from ground engagements between progovernment forces and antigovernment elements.

In May the Taliban announced a spring offensive targeting high-ranking government officials, members of parliament, High Peace Council members, contractors, judges, prosecutors, and others regarded as working against the Taliban's objectives. The Taliban committed four separate attacks against courthouses in Farah, Kabul, Helmand, and Faryab, causing the death of 57 civilians, including judges, prosecutors, and clerical staff. In June the Taliban claimed responsibility for a car bomb that exploded outside the Supreme Court, killing 17 civilians, one of the deadliest attacks in the capital during the year.

The Taliban and other insurgents also killed numerous other civilians. For example, on April 28, the Taliban killed a mullah in his mosque in Nangarhar Province for conducting the funeral of a soldier. Hizb-i-Islami claimed credit for a suicide car bomb attack in Kabul that killed nine civilians on May 16. On August 17, the Taliban attacked a police post in Karokh District of Herat Province, killing 10 civilians and one police officer. The Taliban claimed responsibility for the attack but claimed it killed 11 policemen.

UNAMA reported that improvised explosive devices (IEDs) employed by insurgents continued to be the single largest cause of civilian deaths. Between January and June, there was a 34 percent increase in civilian casualties from IEDs compared with the same period in 2012. Antigovernment elements continued to use suicide attacks to target civilians and government officials.

There were reports of summary justice by the Taliban and other antigovernment elements, including cases resulting in extrajudicial executions. In March two cases of forced amputations by the Taliban in Herat were reported – two drivers of a local transport company were abducted and their hands cut off. Some reports suggested the two men were suspected of stealing, while others indicated they were targeted because their company worked for Western troops.

b. Disappearance

There were reports that insurgent groups were responsible for disappearances and abductions (see section 1.g.). For example, on April 22, after a helicopter made an emergency landing in Logar Province, the Taliban abducted eight Turkish engineers along with the Russian and Kyrgyz flight crew; all those abducted were eventually released.

There were also increased reports of disappearances attributed to security forces, particularly in Kandahar Province. A January UNAMA report on treatment of conflict-related detainees cited credible reports of the alleged disappearance of 81 individuals who were in Afghan National Police (ANP) custody in Kandahar Province. UNAMA also received reports of a large number of unidentified bodies found with gunshot wounds in Kandahar Province.

c. Torture and Other Cruel, Inhuman, or Degrading Treatment or Punishment

Although the constitution prohibits such practices, there were widespread reports that government officials, security forces, detention center authorities, and police committed abuses. NGOs reported that security forces continued to use excessive force, including torturing and beating civilians.

NGOs, UNAMA, and media reports continued to allege that Kandahar provincial chief of police Abdul Raziq facilitated the torture of detainees. UNAMA reported systematic torture at several ANP detention facilities and one Afghan Border

Police Station in Kandahar Province. The Afghanistan Independent Human Rights Commission (AIHRC) found multiple individuals detained by the ANP in Kandahar who claimed mistreatment and torture while in ANP custody. Detainees reportedly were tortured at official and unofficial locations, including ANP check posts, ANP headquarters, and other ANP facilities in Kandahar. Methods of torture included beatings with fists and electric cables; kicking; choking; electric shock; and squeezing of testicles.

UNAMA reported that it found "sufficiently reliable and credible" incidents of torture at 10 National Directorate of Security (NDS) facilities as well as at 15 ANP facilities. For example, UNAMA reported systematic torture at the NDS detention facility in Kandahar Province and NDS Department 124 (counterterrorism) in Kabul. A government delegation assigned to investigate the claims made by UNAMA in its January report also found that officials tortured detainees at NDS Department 124, including with electric shocks, beatings, and threats of sexual violence. During its monitoring visits, the International Security Assistance Force (ISAF) also continued to find instances of torture and abuse of detainees who were held at NDS Department 124. UNAMA also found instances of torture or other mistreatment of detainees held in Afghan National Army (ANA) and ALP custody prior to transfer to the NDS or ANP. Similarly, the government found that 48 percent of detainees interviewed for its investigation (284) had been tortured.

The government created a committee to address allegations of torture emanating from UNAMA's January report on mistreatment of conflict-related detainees, and the committee conducted visits and interviews. The committee, however, did not make its findings public. The government did not hold accountable the perpetrators of torture by conducting credible investigations and prosecutions.

There were some reports that security officials and persons connected to the ANP raped children with impunity. NGOs reported incidents of sexual abuse and exploitation of children by the Afghan National Security Forces (ANSF); however, cultural taboos against reporting such crimes made it difficult to determine the extent of the problem.

UNAMA reported that in February, five men, including two ALP members, raped two boys in Imam Sahib District, Kunduz Province. Authorities arrested the two ALP members in connection with the incident but later released them on bail due to threats made against the victims if they did not withdraw their complaints against the ALP members. According to the national chief of the ALP program, since mid-2012, 88 ALP members had been convicted of human rights violations, such as murder, rape, and mistreatment. These ALP members received sentences ranging from eight to 16 years in prison. A UNAMA report alleged that, in spite of investigations, arrests, and the prosecutions of ALP members involved in human rights abuses, impunity for human rights abuses continued. In July 2012 a complete revetting of all ALP members was initiated; as of March, 100 percent of the partnered units and 90 percent of the total force had been revetted. Approximately 6 percent of ALP members were fired or quit as a result of revetting.

There were reports of abuses of power by "arbakai" (untrained local militia) commanders and their followers. According to UNAMA, many communities used the terms ALP and arbakai interchangeably, making it difficult to confirm reports of abuses by either group. There were credible accounts of murder, rape, assault, the forcible levy of informal taxes, and the traditional practice of "baadh" (the transfer of a girl or woman to another family to settle a debt or grievance) attributed to the ALP. In May arbakai members killed a local mullah in Laghman Province because of public comments he previously made, with which they disagreed.

There were reports of torture and other abuses by the Taliban and other insurgent groups.

Prison and Detention Center Conditions

There were reports of harsh and sometimes life-threatening conditions and abuse in official detention centers, including rape by guards. Different organizations oversaw prisons, juvenile rehabilitation centers, and detention facilities. The General Directorate of Prisons and Detention Centers (GDPDC), part of the Ministry of Interior, has responsibility for all civilian-run prisons – both male and female and civilian detention centers. The Ministry of Justice's Juvenile Rehabilitation Directorate is responsible for all juvenile rehabilitation centers. The ANP, which is under the Ministry of Interior, and the NDS also run short-term detention facilities at the provincial and district levels, usually collocated with their headquarters facility. The Ministry of Defense runs the Afghan National Detention Facilities at Parwan and Pul-e-Charki.

Physical Conditions: The AIHRC and other observers continued to report that inadequate food and water and poor sanitation facilities were common in the prisons. Some observers found the food and water to be sufficient throughout the GDPDC, however. The GDPDC had a nationwide program to feed prisoners but was on an extremely limited budget. Many prisoners' families provided food supplements and other necessary items.

There were 34 provincial prisons under GDPDC control, 187 active Ministry of Interior detention facilities, and 30 juvenile rehabilitation centers. The total number of active detention facilities reportedly fluctuated from month to month. Overall, the Ministry of Interior lacked sufficient detention facilities. No official information was available on the number of NDS prisoners or NDS-operated facilities.

Authorities generally did not have the infrastructure capacity to separate pretrial and posttrial inmates. As of the end of the year, the GDPDC reported 7,232 male pretrial detainees, 20,888 male prisoners, 133 female pretrial detainees, and 721 female prisoners. In most instances limited infrastructure hindered housing prisoners by their classification, but where it was feasible the GDPDC did so. Women were not imprisoned with men. Authorities generally did not have the infrastructure capacity to separate juveniles based on the nature of the charges against them.

Under the law children younger than seven may live with their mothers in prison. This practice, however, was reduced significantly under the direction of the GDPDC and in conjunction with the opening of some children's support centers. Reports indicated that the children placed in the support centers were thriving in this new environment and that, even after being released, some mothers requested that their children remain in the centers due to improved education and health services.

Administration: There was an informal grievance procedure within the GDPDC. The Ministry of Justice, the attorney general, and some governors monitored or assessed prison conditions, but investigations and monitoring did not fully meet international standards. In January a delegation comprising representatives from the Independent Commission on Oversight of the Implementation of the Constitution, legal academics from Kabul University, and legal advisors from the Office of the President, the Ministry of Interior, and the NDS visited prisons and detention centers in Kabul, Kandahar, and Herat as part of a "fact finding delegation on existence of torture and abuse in prisons, detention centers, and jails" mandated by Presidential Order 6673. The delegation's findings on torture in prisons and detention centers led President Karzai to issue a decree directing government agencies to take measures designed to improve the legal process and physical conditions for incarcerated individuals. A formal prisoner complaint process was outlined under a 2012 GDPDC directive, but it was not in place at year's end. Although the practice varied by prison, commanders designated certain inmates to report back to them on security and internal situations. In 2011 the NDS established a human rights unit to investigate claims of detainee mistreatment and take action against perpetrators of abuse. Human rights observers complained that the progress and effectiveness of the unit was limited. ISAF worked to bolster the resources and effectiveness of this organization through partnering with ISAF detention monitoring teams and the AIHRC.

The law provides prisoners with the right to leave prison for up to 20 days for visits. This right, however, was not respected in most prisons, and the law is unclear in its application to different classes of prisoners. At GDPDC and Juvenile Rehabilitation Directorate correctional facilities, inmates were able to receive visitors on a regular basis.

Provisions for alternatives to incarceration were rarely utilized in practice. Regular presidential pardons on holidays were the only practice that diverted inmates from prison.

In government detention facilities, observers reported that prisoners were permitted religious observance.

Independent Monitoring: The AIHRC, UNAMA, the International Committee of the Red Cross (ICRC), and ISAF generally were provided access to Ministry of Interior, Ministry of Justice, NDS, and Ministry of Defense (MOD) detention facilities. Security constraints and obstruction by some authorities occasionally prevented visits to some places of detention. UNAMA and the AIHRC reported difficultly accessing NDS places of detention unannounced. Despite multiple announcements throughout the year that human rights organizations would have unimpeded access to NDS places of detention, both organizations reported that access was repeatedly denied or delayed throughout the country, but particularly at facilities in Kabul and Kandahar. While ISAF did not experience the same level of difficultly, unannounced access was denied on several occasions at both NDS and ANP facilities. The AIHRC reported that, before visiting detention facilities, NDS officials usually required the AIHRC to submit a formal letter requesting access at least one to two days in advance. NDS officials continued to prohibit AIHRC and UNAMA monitors from bringing cameras into NDS facilities, thereby preventing AIHRC monitors from properly documenting physical evidence of abuse, such as bruises, scars, and other injuries. In February two members of parliament investigating claims of torture at prisons in Kandahar were barred from access to prisons on the order of the provincial governor.

There were multiple reports of "secret" or undeclared detention facilities run by Kandahar provincial chief of police Abdul Raziq in Kandahar Province, set up specifically to avoid international monitors.

d. Arbitrary Arrest or Detention

The law prohibits arbitrary arrest or detention, but both remained serious problems. Authorities detained many citizens without respecting essential procedural protections.

According to NGOs, law enforcement officers continued to arbitrarily detain citizens without clear legal authority and due process. Local law enforcement officials reportedly detained persons illegally on charges not provided for in the penal code and used their official status to resolve petty disputes. The Attorney General's Office ordered a halt to arrests and convictions for "running away," which is not a crime under the law. Reports indicated, however, that prosecutors instead charged women who had left home with "attempted adultery" for being outside the home in the perceived presence of nonrelated men. In some cases women who had left home were imprisoned because it was unsafe for them to return home and there was no shelter available elsewhere (see section 6).

Role of the Police and Security Apparatus

Three ministries have responsibility both in law and in practice for providing security in the country. The ANP and the ALP, under the Ministry of Interior, have primary responsibility for internal order but also were engaged in fighting the insurgency internally. The ANA, under the Ministry of Defense, is responsible for external security but was fighting the insurgency internally as well. The NDS has responsibility for investigating criminal cases concerning national security and also functions as an intelligence agency. The investigative branch of the NDS operated a facility in Kabul, where it held prisoners on a pretrial basis until their cases were handed over to prosecutors. In some areas insurgents rather than the ANP or ANA maintained control.

There were reports of official impunity and lack of accountability throughout the year. Observers stated that ALP and ANP personnel were largely unaware of their responsibilities and defendants' rights under the law. According to UNAMA, accountability of NDS and ANP officials for torture and abuse was weak, not transparent, and rarely enforced. There was limited independent judicial, or external oversight of the NDS and ANP as institutions or investigation and prosecution of crimes or misconduct committed by NDS and ANP officials, including torture and abuse.

International support for recruiting and training new ANP personnel continued, with the goal of professionalizing the police force. The international community worked with the government to develop and offer human rights awareness and police training programs. In addition to core policing skills and internal investigation mechanisms to curb security force corruption and abuses, these programs emphasized law enforcement, the constitution, values and ethics, professional development, the prevention of domestic violence, and fundamental standards of human rights.

Nevertheless, human rights problems persisted, and observers criticized the inadequate preparation and lack of sensitivity of local security forces. Human rights institutions expressed concerns about the limited oversight and accountability that existed for security institutions, especially the ALP, although the Ministry of Interior took some measures at the end of the year to increase accountability of the ALP. For example, the Ministry of Interior worked with the ICRC to increase human rights training for ALP recruits.

NGOs and human rights activists noted that societal violence, especially against women, was widespread. In many cases police did not prevent or respond to the violence and in some cases arrested women who reported crimes committed against them, such as rape.

Arrest Procedures and Treatment of Detainees

Arbitrary Arrest: Arbitrary arrest and detention remained a problem.

Pretrial Detention: The law provides for access to legal counsel and the use of warrants, and it limits how long detainees may be held without charge. Police have the right to detain a suspect for 72 hours to complete a preliminary investigation. If they decide to pursue a case, the file is transferred to the Attorney General's Office, which must interrogate the suspect within 48 hours. The investigating prosecutor can continue to detain a suspect without formal charges for 15 days from the time of arrest while continuing the investigation. With court approval the investigating prosecutor may detain a suspect for an additional 15 days. The prosecutor must file an indictment or release the suspect within 30 days of arrest. An investigation may continue even if an indictment cannot be completed within the 30 days. UNAMA, the ICRC, the AIHRC, and other observers reported that arbitrary and prolonged detention frequently occurred throughout the country. Authorities often did not inform detainees of the charges against them.

Many detainees did not benefit from any or all of these provisions, largely due to a lack of resources, limited numbers of defense attorneys, unskilled legal practitioners, and corruption. The law provides that, upon request by defense counsel, the court must release a detainee held beyond the 30-day period when an indictment is not filed. Many detainees, however, were held beyond 30 days, despite the lack of an indictment. Observers reported that some prosecutors and police detained individuals without charging them for actions that were not crimes under the law, in part because the judicial system was inadequate to process detainees in a timely fashion.

The seven government entities involved in the criminal justice sector – the Ministry of Justice, the Attorney General's Office, the Supreme Court, the Ministry of Interior, the NDS, the Ministry of Defense and the High Office of Oversight – continued to implement a standard case management system.

Arbitrary arrests were reported in most provinces. Incommunicado imprisonment remained a problem, and prompt access to a lawyer was rare. While prisoners were allowed access to their families, there were many cases in which such access was not prompt. Some detainees were subjected to torture and other mistreatment, including being whipped, exposed to extreme cold, and deprived of food. On September 15, a video on Facebook depicted individuals who appeared to be ANSF members whipping a detainee. UNAMA reported that police also detained individuals for moral crimes, breach of contract, family disputes, and to extract confessions. Observers reported that those detained for moral crimes were almost exclusively women. The criminal code prescribes penalties for some sexual behavior and contractual violations. There was little consistency in the length of time detainees were held before trial or arraignment. Detention after sentencing also was reportedly common.

In September 2012 authorities arrested two Philippine citizens because their foreign employer allegedly failed to pay for goods and services it had received from Afghan subcontractors. When government authorities could not locate any senior managers of the company, they initially detained 20 employees as collateral for the alleged debt. After being held without charge for more than a year with no opportunity to contest their detention, the two Philippine men were brought before a judge in October. The two were released in November following diplomatic engagement with Afghan officials. The case was one of many in which the Attorney General's Office, with the complicity of some police officials, imposed or threatened to impose criminal penalties on persons who may only be indirectly connected to a contractual dispute with an Afghan person or entity. The arrest of employees to collect an alleged debt of their employer under a commercial contract is inconsistent with the constitution as well as international legal obligations under the International Covenant on Civil and Political Rights.

As of June 20, according to the Ministry of Justice, 173 children were detained on national security-related charges in juvenile rehabilitation centers. The juvenile code presumes that children should not be held to the same standards as adults. The code states that the arrest of a child "should be a matter of last resort and should last for the shortest possible period." Reports indicated that children in juvenile rehabilitation centers across the country lacked access to adequate food, health care, and education. Detained children typically were denied basic rights and many aspects of due process, including the presumption of innocence, the right to be informed of charges, access to defense lawyers, and the right not to be forced to confess. The law provides for the creation of juvenile police, prosecution offices, and courts. Due to limited resources, special juvenile courts functioned in only six areas (Kabul, Herat, Balkh, Kandahar, Jalalabad, and Kunduz). In provinces where special courts do not exist, children's cases fall under the ordinary courts. The law also mandates that children's cases be addressed in private and, like all criminal cases, may involve three stages: primary, appeals, and the final stage at the Supreme Court.

Some of the children in the criminal justice system were victims rather than perpetrators of crime. Particularly in cases of sexual exploitation, perpetrators were seldom prosecuted or imprisoned. Some victims were perceived as shameful and in need of punishment because they brought shame on their family by reporting an abuse. In some cases abused children were imprisoned because they could not return to their families and shelter elsewhere was unavailable. Some children related to a perpetrator allegedly were imprisoned as a family proxy for the actual perpetrator.

"Zina" is the term in Afghan law for extramarital sexual relations. Police and legal officials often charged women with intent to commit zina to justify their arrest and incarceration for social offenses, such as running away from home, defying family choice of a spouse, fleeing domestic violence or rape, or eloping. Article 130 of the constitution provides courts with the discretion to use sharia (Islamic law) through the Hanafi school of Islamic jurisprudence to dispense justice in cases not covered by the constitution, penal code, or other laws. Observers reported that legal officials used this article to charge women and men with "immorality" or "running away from home." Police often detained women for zina at the request of family members.

Authorities imprisoned some women for reporting crimes perpetrated against them and some as proxies serving as substitutes for their husbands or male relatives convicted of crimes. The AIHRC received reports of men being arrested in place of a male relative when a suspect could not be located, on the assumption that the suspect would turn himself in to free the family member.

Authorities placed some women in protective custody to prevent violent retaliation by family members. Authorities also placed women who were victims of domestic violence in protective custody (including in a detention center) if there was no shelter facility available to protect them from further abuse. Under the 2009 Law on the Elimination of Violence against Women (EVAW), police have the obligation to arrest persons who abuse women. Implementation and awareness of the EVAW law was limited, however.

Authorities frequently did not re-arrest defendants, even after an appellate court convicted them in absentia. There was no bond system, although a rudimentary personal recognizance system was utilized in some areas where international observers monitored cases. Authorities justified posttrial detention because defendants released pending appeal often disappeared.

Prosecutors did not exercise discretion in making decisions on charges. International mentors observed that prosecutors filed indictments in cases transferred to them by police, even where there was a reasonable belief that no crime was actually committed.

Amnesty: Contrary to some misconceptions, the Afghanistan Peace and Reintegration Program (APRP) is a mechanism for bringing combatants off the battlefield and does not provide amnesty for criminal activity unrelated to the insurgency. The program document states that the APRP "is not a framework for pardoning all crimes and providing blanket amnesty," and reintegration candidates are informed prior to enrollment that entry into the program does not amount to blanket immunity from prosecution.

e. Denial of Fair Public Trial

The law provides for an independent judiciary, but the judiciary continued to be underfunded, understaffed, inadequately trained, ineffective, and subject to threats, bias, political influence, and pervasive corruption. For example, the Supreme Court chief justice and three associate justices continued to serve as "acting justices" beyond the expiration of their constitutionally mandated term limits. Two new justices were nominated by President Karzai toward the end of the year and confirmed by parliament on December 25. The delay in the appointments was widely regarded as an executive branch effort to maintain its influence and control over the judiciary. Bribery, corruption, and pressure from public officials, tribal leaders, families of accused persons, and individuals associated with the insurgency continued to impair judicial impartiality. Most courts administered justice unevenly, according to a mixture of codified law, sharia , and local custom. Traditional justice mechanisms remained the main recourse for many, especially in rural areas. There was varying adherence to codified law, with courts disregarding applicable statutory law in favor of sharia or local custom. According to a 2012 Freedom House report, the Supreme Court was primarily composed of religious scholars who had limited knowledge of civil jurisprudence.

The formal justice system was relatively strong in urban centers, where the central government was strongest, and weaker in rural areas, where approximately 80 percent of the population lived. Courts, police forces, and prisons continued to operate at less than full capacity nationwide. The judicial system continued to lack the capacity to handle the large volume of new and amended legislation. A lack of qualified judicial personnel hindered the courts. Some municipal and provincial authorities, including judges, had minimal training and often based their judgments on their personal understanding of sharia, without appropriate reference to statutory law, tribal codes of honor, or local custom. Compared with 2012, there was an increase during the year in the number of judges who were graduates of law school, many from universities with sharia faculties. Access to legal codes and statutes increased, but their limited availability continued to hinder some judges and prosecutors.

There were widespread shortages of judges, primarily in insecure areas. UNAMA documented targeted killings of judges across the country, including in Farah Province. District prosecutors faced similar threats and were killed in Logar and Farah provinces. The Supreme Court reported that as of August there were an estimated 1,820 judges at the primary, appellate, and Supreme Court levels, including 152 female judges.

In major cities, courts continued to decide criminal cases as mandated by law. Civil cases continued to be frequently resolved in the informal system or, in some cases, pursuant to negotiations facilitated by formal justice system actors or private lawyers. Because the formal legal system often was not present in rural areas, local elders and shuras (consultative gatherings, usually of men selected by the community) were the primary means of settling both criminal matters and civil disputes and also levied unsanctioned punishments. Some estimates suggested that 80 percent of all disputes were resolved by shuras/jirgas. In some cases shuras violated the rights of women and minorities.

In some areas the Taliban enforced a parallel judicial system based on strict interpretation of sharia. For example, in February the Taliban ordered a woman to be publicly whipped 40 times for alleged sexual relations with a man before being expelled from western Ghor Province. In some cases punishments imposed included execution or mutilation.

Trial Procedures

Trial procedures rarely met internationally accepted standards. The administration and implementation of justice varied in different areas of the country. The government formally utilizes an inquisitorial legal system. By law all citizens are entitled to a presumption of innocence and those accused have the right to be present at trial and to appeal, although these rights were not always applied. In some provinces public trials were held, but this was not the norm. Judges decided criminal trials because there is no right to a jury trial under the constitution. An indigent defendant has the right to consult with an advocate or counsel at public expense when resources allow. This right was applied inconsistently, in large part due to a severe shortage of defense counsel. Citizens often were unaware of their constitutional rights. Defendants and attorneys were entitled to examine the physical evidence and the documents related to their case before trial, although observers noted that court documents often were not available for review before cases went to trial, despite defense lawyers' requests.

In general criminal defense attorneys reported that justice system officials were slowly demonstrating increased respect for and tolerance of the role of defense lawyers in criminal trials. Criminal defense attorneys, however, were sometimes subjected to abusive and threatening treatment by prosecutors and other law enforcement officials. For example, an NGO reported that in Laghman Province an Attorney General's Office prosecutor threatened a lawyer who objected to legal violations committed by the NDS in a criminal matter with possible prosecution for criminal association with antigovernment elements.

When the accused is held in custody, the primary court must render a verdict within 60 days. The appellate court has two months to review the case of an incarcerated person. Either side may appeal; a decision is not final until reviewed by all three levels of the judiciary. An accused defendant who is found innocent usually remains detained in the legal system until the case moves through all three levels: primary, appeals, and the Supreme Court. The decision of the primary court becomes final if an appeal is not filed within 20 days. Any second appeal must be filed within 30 days, after which the case moves to the Supreme Court, which must decide the case of the defendant within 60 days. If the appellate deadlines are not met, the law requires that the accused be released from custody. In many cases courts did not meet these deadlines.

In cases lacking a clearly defined legal statute, or cases in which judges, prosecutors, or elders were unaware of the law, judges and informal shuras enforced customary law; this practice often resulted in outcomes that discriminated against women. The practice of baadh – in which young girls were offered as compensation to families whom defendants had wronged – reportedly continued in some instances.

Political Prisoners and Detainees

There were no reports that the government held political prisoners or detainees.

Civil Judicial Procedures and Remedies

Citizens had limited access to justice for constitutional and human rights violations, and interpretations of religious doctrine in some cases took precedence over human rights or constitutional rights. The state judiciary did not play a significant or effective role in adjudicating civil matters due to corruption and lack of capacity, although the judiciary adjudicated family law matters with some frequency.

f. Arbitrary Interference with Privacy, Family, Home, or Correspondence

The law prohibits arbitrary interference in matters of privacy. The government did not respect these prohibitions, and there were no legal protections for victims.

Government officials continued to forcibly enter homes and businesses of civilians without legal authorization, although, according to UNAMA, there was a reduction in such instances.

Authorities imprisoned men and women as substitutes for male relatives who were suspects or convicted criminals in order to induce those persons at large to surrender themselves (see section 1.d.).

Insurgents continued to intimidate mobile telephone operators to shut down operations. Reports of destruction of mobile telephone towers, bribing of guards, and disconnecting networks at night were particularly common in the southwestern, southern, and eastern provinces.

g. Use of Excessive Force and Other Abuses in Internal Conflicts

Continuing internal conflict resulted in civilian deaths, abductions, prisoner abuse, property damage, displacement of residents, and other abuses. The security situation remained a problem during the year due to insurgent attacks. Civilians continued to bear the brunt of intensified armed conflict, particularly women and children, according to UNAMA. Civilian deaths between January and June increased by 14 percent compared with the same period in 2012. The vast majority of civilian deaths were caused by antigovernment elements.

Killings: Government and progovernment forces were responsible for civilian casualties. The UNAMA midyear *Report on the Protection of Citizens in Armed Conflict* stated that the progovernment forces were responsible for 9 percent of total civilian casualties (362 total), which represented a 16 percent increase compared with the first half of 2012. The UNAMA report indicated that, on May 5, an ALP member killed a civilian in Dasht-e-Archi District of Kunduz Province.

UNAMA noted that antigovernment elements were responsible for 74 percent of civilian casualties in the first half of the year, a 16 percent increase compared with the same period in 2012.

Antigovernment elements continued to attack religious leaders who they concluded spoke against the insurgency or the Taliban. Antigovernment elements also continued to target government officials and forces. Statistics showed that casualties for the ALP, ANP, and ANA more than doubled during the year. UNAMA also reported that antigovernment elements sometimes used civilian residences to launch attacks against progovernment forces, which prompted return fire and additional civilian casualties.

The Taliban and antigovernment elements continued to engage in indiscriminate use of force, attacking and killing villagers, foreigners, and NGO workers in attacks and with car bombs and suicide bombs. IED attacks killed more civilians than any other tactic during the year, accounting for 34 percent of all civilian casualties in the first half of the year.

Abductions: The Ministry of Interior's Anticrime Police reported 102 abductions during 2012, as the Taliban targeted construction and mining projects, teachers, and citizens perceived to be cooperating with the international community (see section 1.b.). The actual number of cases may have been much higher, and this trend continued during the year.

Physical Abuse, Punishment, and Torture: Land mines and unexploded ordnance continued to cause deaths and injuries, restrict areas available for farming, and impede the return of refugees. The Mine Action Coordination Center for Afghanistan (MACCA) reported that deaths and injuries from land mines and unexploded ordnance remained consistent with previous years. In 2010-11, an average of 42 persons were killed or injured each month. This average continued, with 123 reported victims during the first quarter of the year. In addition to these casualties from traditional antitank and antipersonnel mines, there continued to be thousands of civilian casualties from IEDs. According to the MACCA, land mines and unexploded ordnance imperiled 31,847 communities, which represented approximately 11 percent of total communities. The majority of remaining mine hazard areas included a relatively low number of arbitrarily placed mines dispersed over a large area but that nonetheless denied full use of the land to communities. The Ministry of Education and NGOs continued to conduct educational programs and mine awareness campaigns throughout the country.

Child Soldiers: The government, with international assistance, officially vetted all recruits into the armed forces and police, rejecting applicants under the age of 18. There were reports, however, that children were recruited and used for military purposes by the ANSF and progovernment militias. UNAMA documented 16 incidents of recruitment of children into antigovernment armed groups and the ANSF in the first half of the year. Within this figure, at least seven children were recruited by the ALP, one by the ANP, and 23 by the Taliban and other antigovernment elements. In some cases reports indicated that children altered national identity cards to indicate an age of 18 or older in order to pass official vetting procedures. The media also reported that in some cases ANSF units used children as personal servants or support staff, particularly for sexual purposes.

UNAMA also documented recruitment of children into armed groups. The Taliban and other antigovernment elements recruited at least 23 children. In some cases the Taliban and other antigovernment elements used children as suicide bombers and human shields and in other cases to assist with their work, such as placing IEDs, particularly in southern provinces. The media, NGOs, and UN agencies reported that the Taliban tricked children, promised them money, used false religious pretexts, or forced them to become suicide bombers.

Also see the Department of State's annual *Trafficking in Persons Report* at www.state.gov/j/tip/.

Other Conflict-related Abuses

The security environment continued to have a negative effect on the ability of humanitarian organizations to operate freely in many parts of the country. Insurgents deliberately targeted government employees and aid workers.

Suspected Taliban members fired on NGO vehicles and attacked NGO offices, guest houses, and hotels frequented by NGO employees. Violence and instability hampered development, relief, and reconstruction efforts. NGOs reported that insurgents, powerful local individuals, and militia leaders demanded bribes to allow groups to bring relief supplies into the country and distribute them. UNAMA documented 12 attacks on hospitals and medical staff in the first half of the year.

In August in Herat, the Taliban kidnapped and killed five Afghan employees of the International Rescue Committee and a foreign aid organization that had been in the country since 1988. A sixth victim worked for the Ministry of Rural Rehabilitation and Development.

The Taliban continued to distribute threatening messages in attempts to curtail government and development activities. Insurgents used civilians, including children, as human shields, either by forcing them into the line of fire or by basing operations in civilian settings.

In the south and east, the Taliban and other antigovernment elements frequently forced local residents to provide food and shelter for their fighters. The Taliban also continued to attack schools, radio stations, and government offices.

On May 29, a group of four suicide bombers attacked the ICRC office in Jalalabad. One of the bombers blew himself up at the front door of the building, killing a guard. Security forces responded and killed the remaining attackers. The Taliban issued a statement denying involvement. As of year's end, no group had taken credit for the attack.

Section 2. Respect for Civil Liberties, Including:

a. Freedom of Speech and Press

The constitution provides for freedom of speech and of the press, but the government restricted these rights.

Freedom of Speech: Authorities used pressure, regulations, and threats to silence critics. Politicians, security officials, and others in positions of power arrested, threatened, or harassed a growing number of journalists as a result of their coverage. Freedom of speech and an independent media were even more constrained at the provincial level, where many media outlets were linked to specific personalities or political parties, including local power brokers, such as former mujahedeen-era military leaders who owned many of the broadcasting stations and print media and influenced their content. Many local warlords did not tolerate independent media in their provinces.

Press Freedoms: Despite obstacles, print media continued to publish independent magazines, newsletters, and newspapers, although circulation was low. A wide range of editorials and dailies openly criticized the government. Due to high levels of illiteracy, however, most citizens preferred television or radio over print media. Radio remained more widespread due to its relative accessibility, with 81 percent radio penetration, compared to 42 percent for television and 13 percent for print.

In 2012 the Ministry of Information and Culture presented a draft media law for public comment, with the goal of replacing the 2009 Mass Media Law. Local and international analysts roundly criticized the draft, arguing that it would increase government control over media and introduce new restrictions on press freedoms, such as special courts. At the beginning of the year, the draft law apparently was blocked by public opposition, but in July the debate to replace the 2009 law resumed, as journalists and the Ministry of Information and Culture quarreled over implementation of the law. The minister introduced amendments to the 2009 law that would grant him expanded power to refer cases for criminal prosecution if he found specific speech to be offensive. In September the lower house of parliament overwhelmingly approved the amendments, but the upper house had not voted as of year's end.

The Ministry of Information and Culture has the authority to regulate the press and media but by year's end had not created the Mass Media Commission required by the law to exercise that authority. Unlike in previous years, there were no confirmed reports that the government directly sought to restrict the ministry's operations. While the ministry is legally responsible for regulating media, the council of religious scholars (the Ulama Council) had considerable influence over media affairs. In November the Independent Election Commission (IEC) formed its own Media Commission to regulate both print and broadcast media coverage of presidential and provincial council candidates ahead of the legal campaign period that would begin in 2014. On December 30, the IEC's Media Commission issued regulations for the media to follow in the upcoming elections. These rules appeared to ban coverage of polling and other activities, including criticism of any of the announced candidates in the precampaign period. The media criticized them.

Violence and Harassment: Authorities regularly used threats, violence, and intimidation to silence opposition journalists, particularly those who spoke out about impunity, war crimes, government officials, and powerful local figures. For example, in July authorities arrested a reporter at the *Mandegar Daily* for writing an article about corruption in the High Office of Oversight and Anticorruption (HOO), the government organ responsible for mitigating corruption. In response to the article, the head of the HOO reportedly demanded that the Attorney General's Office arrest the journalist, who was held in custody for 10 days before being released on bail. The case was not resolved by year's end.

Prevailing security conditions created a dangerous environment for journalists, even when they were not targeted specifically. In a number of instances, crowds attacked and beat journalists who were reporting on demonstrations against the government. Nai Media Watch reported an increase in incidents of violence and threats against journalists and at year's end reported that nearly 70 percent of the cases could be attributed to the government or someone in the government. For example, on July 27, the governor of Parwan and his bodyguards confronted a journalist and beat him with a bottle in a Kabul restaurant after the journalist criticized the governor on Facebook.

An independent journalist safety organization continued to operate a safe house for journalists facing threats. It reported that law enforcement officials generally cooperated in providing assistance to journalists with credible fear, although limited investigative capacity meant many cases remained unresolved. The Afghan Independent Bar Association established a media law committee to provide legal support, expertise, and services to media bodies.

The number of female journalists remained low. Female reporters found it difficult to practice their profession, although some women oversaw radio stations across the country, and some radio stations were devoted to women's issues. Factors such as poor security, lack of access to training, and unsafe working conditions continued to limit the participation of women in the media. The Afghan Journalists Safety Committee also reported that female reporters often were subjected to sexual abuse by media managers.

Censorship or Content Restrictions: The government reportedly sought to censor the media directly or indirectly and restrict reporting on topics deemed contrary to the government messaging. On August 2, the Ministry of Interior and the NDS reportedly pressured the Pajhwok News Agency to remove a report from its website that criticized the ANP leadership for the high number of ANP casualties in a police operation.

Some media observers claimed that journalists self-censored reporting on administrative corruption, land embezzlement, and local officials' involvement in narcotics trafficking due to fear of violent retribution by provincial police officials and powerful families. Because of such pressures, media outlets often preferred to quote from foreign media reports on sensitive cases and in some cases fed stories to foreign journalists.

Libel Laws/National Security: The penal code and the 2009 Mass Media Law prescribe jail sentences and fines for defamation. Defamation sometimes was used as a pretext to suppress criticism of government officials. In May the Attorney General's Office initiated an investigation of the daily newspaper *Hasht-e-Sobh* after it published a report on extensive corruption and nepotism at the Ministry of Mines. The Attorney General's Office claimed defamation, but the case was not reviewed first by the Ministry of Information and Culture, as required by law.

<u>Nongovernmental Impact</u>: Journalists continued to face threats from the Taliban and other insurgents. Reporters acknowledged that they avoided criticizing the insurgency and some neighboring countries in their reporting because they feared Taliban retribution. Violence and intimidation of journalists, reporters, and media by insurgent forces and the Taliban remained concerns and continued to restrict journalists' operating space.

The Taliban manipulated the media, especially print journalism, both directly and indirectly, by threatening to harm some journalists physically and by directly feeding news to others. Journalists reported receiving threats if they published stories favorable to the government.

The Committee to Protect Journalists reported that local and foreign reporters continued to risk kidnapping.

Internet Freedom

There were credible reports that the government restricted access to the internet. In June 2012 the Ministry of Telecommunications announced its intent to filter pornographic content and gambling websites but continued to lack the capacity to enforce the directive during the year.

The Taliban also used the internet and social media (e.g., Twitter) to spread its messages. Although internet coverage was high, usage remained low due to high prices, inadequate local content, and illiteracy.

Academic Freedom and Cultural Events

The government imposed restrictions on curricula and research it deemed un-Islamic, requiring prior approval of "concerned ministries and institutions," such as the Ministry of Hajj and Religious Affairs. Conservative lawmakers criticized what they believed to be "vulgar and un-Islamic" television programs, such as the *Voice of Afghanistan*, and demanded, unsuccessfully, that the Ministry of Information and Culture ban "anti-Islamic broadcasts." Female singers and actresses faced regular death threats.

b. Freedom of Peaceful Assembly and Association

Freedom of Assembly

The government generally respected citizens' rights to demonstrate peacefully. There were numerous public gatherings or protests during the year related to a variety of causes, including corruption, civilian casualties, and violence against women. In May when the parliament brought up the EVAW law for public debate, more than 700 Kabul University students took to the streets. They called the law un-Islamic and, carrying green and white flags, asserted they would join the Taliban against the government if the law was not repealed. Days later, dozens of women took to the street in a counterprotest, demanding that the law remain in force.

Freedom of Association

The 2009 law on political parties obliges parties to register with the Ministry of Justice and to pursue objectives consistent with Islam. The law raised the hurdles for registration of parties, requiring at least 10,000 registered members.

In April 2012 the Council of Ministers approved a regulation that requires political parties to open offices in at least 20 provinces within one year of registration, warning that parties that failed to comply would be removed from the Ministry of Justice's official list. During a nationwide review during the year of provincial political party offices, the Ministry of Justice found various political parties not in compliance with the regulation but did not deregister any political party by year's end.

c. Freedom of Religion

See the Department of State's *International Religious Freedom Report* at www.state.gov/j/drl/irf/rpt/.

d. Freedom of Movement, Internally Displaced Persons, Protection of Refugees, and Stateless Persons

The law provides for freedom of internal movement, foreign travel, emigration, and repatriation, but the government sometimes limited citizens' movement for security reasons.

The government continued to cooperate with the UN High Commissioner for Refugees (UNHCR), the International Organization for Migration, and other humanitarian organizations in providing protection and assistance to internally displaced persons, refugees, returning refugees, and other persons of concern.

Government assistance to vulnerable persons, including returnees from Pakistan and Iran, remained low, with a continued reliance on the international community.

In-country Movement: Taxi, truck, and bus drivers reported that security forces operated illegal checkpoints and extorted money and goods from travelers.

The greatest barrier to movement in some parts of the country was the lack of security. In many areas insurgent violence, banditry, land mines, and IEDs made travel extremely dangerous, especially at night.

Armed insurgents also operated illegal checkpoints and extorted money and goods. The Taliban imposed nightly curfews on the local populace in regions where it exercised authority, mostly in the southeast.

Social custom limited women's freedom of movement without male consent or a male chaperone.

Internally Displaced Persons (IDPs)

Internal population movements increased, mainly triggered by military operations, as well as by natural disasters and irregular labor conditions. According to the UNHCR, at the end of August an estimated 590,184 persons were internally displaced due to conflict in the country. Armed conflict and hostilities, the general deterioration of security, threats and intimidation, and military operations were cited as the major specific causes of displacement. More than half of all IDPs resided in the four provinces of Herat, Nangarhar, Helmand, and Kandahar, according to the Internal Displacement Monitoring Center.

Through September authorities recorded 113,241 new conflict-induced displaced persons. During this same period, the regional IDP task forces that undertook interagency assessments to ascertain needs assisted 87,093 conflict-induced IDPs with nonfood items.

Limited humanitarian access caused delays in identification, assessment, and timely assistance to IDPs, leading to estimates that the number of IDPs was significantly larger than official government figures. IDPs continued to lack access to basic protection, including personal and physical security and shelter. IDPs in urban areas reportedly faced discrimination, inadequate sanitation and other basic services, and lived in constant risk of eviction from illegally occupied displacement sites, according to the Internal Displacement Monitoring Center.

Women in IDP camps reported high levels of domestic violence. There were limited opportunities to earn a livelihood during displacement, which led to secondary displacement, making tracking of vulnerable persons difficult. IDPs usually had access to local social services, but some areas were distant from schools and other services.

Protection of Refugees

Access to Asylum: Laws do not provide for granting asylum or refugee status, and the government has not established a system for providing protection to refugees. In accordance with international protocols and agreement between Afghanistan, Pakistan, and the UNHCR, repatriation to Afghanistan must be voluntary.

The government continued to provide protection against the expulsion or return of refugees to countries where their lives or freedom would be threatened on account of their race, religion, nationality, membership in a particular social group, or political opinion.

The government's capacity to absorb returned refugees remained low. Although the UNHCR reported that economic and security difficulties in Pakistan and Iran had led to the increased return of Afghan refugees in 2012, the number of refugees returning decreased during the year due to uncertainty about security in the posttransition period.

During the year more than 30,000 Afghan refugees voluntarily repatriated with UNHCR assistance. The average number of returns per day reflected a 40 percent decrease from the same period in 2012.

Access to Basic Services: Resettlement of returnees remained difficult. The UNHCR, in conjunction with the governments of Afghanistan, Iran, and Pakistan, developed a strategy aimed at preserving refugee status for those remaining in neighboring countries while assisting with the reintegration of returnees through targeted assistance, including educational, health, and employment assistance. Returnees ostensibly had equal access to health, education, and other services, although some areas with large populations of returning refugees had limited means of transportation or lacked roads leading to larger, more established villages and urban centers, which made access to such services and economic opportunities difficult.

Section 3. Respect for Political Rights: The Right of Citizens to Change Their Government

The constitution provides citizens the right to change their government peacefully, and citizens exercised this right in the 2010 parliamentary elections based on universal suffrage. The elections were marred by serious widespread fraud and corruption, however. The parliamentary elections were disputed for nearly a year after President Karzai established an unconstitutional special elections tribunal to investigate the election results. In 2011 the president issued a decree acknowledging that the IEC was the sole authority to resolve the electoral impasse. In July President Karzai signed two new laws passed by parliament establishing a strengthened electoral framework prior to the 2014 presidential and provincial council elections.

Elections and Political Participation

Recent Elections: The September 2010 parliamentary elections were held amid significant security and logistical challenges. Widespread fraud and corruption hampered the elections, particularly at the subnational level. International observers and civil society groups documented instances of ballot stuffing, ghost polling stations, and some interference by staff of electoral bodies and security forces. Fraud was especially notable in areas with high levels of insecurity, limited observer and candidate agent coverage, and insufficient female electoral staff. In response to protests about the election results, in December 2010 President Karzai appointed a special tribunal to investigate and recommend changes to the election results. The IEC, parliamentarians, and NGOs challenged the legality and constitutionality of the special tribunal, calling for its dissolution. The creation of the special tribunal resulted in a political impasse that virtually halted legislative action until June 2011.

While security preparations improved relative to the 2009 presidential election, security was still inadequate in many locations, and numerous irregularities occurred, including intimidation of voters, polling staff, and candidates, especially women.

In 2009 citizens voted in their second contested presidential election. The IEC declared Karzai president for a second term, after his challenger, Abdullah Abdullah, withdrew from a runoff election. The elections were similarly marred by allegations of widespread fraud.

Political Parties: Negative associations with violent militia groups and the former communist regime, as well as allegations of persistent corruption and inefficiency, led many citizens to view political parties with suspicion. The 2009 Party Law granted parties the right to exist as formal institutions for the first time in the country's history. The Party Law requires parties to have at least 10,000 members from a minimum of 22 provinces. After parliament passed the law in 2009, many political parties complained that they had very little time to complete the registration process in advance of the 2010 parliamentary elections. The National Democratic Institute reported that a number of parties alleged that the Ministry of Justice, responsible for the registration of political parties, engaged in fraud and treated parties unequally.

Political parties were not always able to conduct activities throughout the country, particularly in regions where antigovernment violence affected overall security. Violence against participants in the political party system was common, even during nonelection periods. As of August 18, there were 56 political parties registered with the Ministry of Justice. In April 2012 the Council of Ministers approved a regulation requiring political parties to open offices in at least 20 provinces within one year of registration, warning that parties that failed to comply would be removed from the ministry's official list.

According to Ministry of Justice officials, a deregistered party would still be able to meet and continue "informal" political activities, but candidates for political office could not run under the party's name. During a nationwide review of provincial political party offices during the year, the Ministry of Justice found various political parties not in compliance with the regulation but did not publicly announce the deregistration of any party. Provincial party members asserted that the ministry's monitoring process was uneven, with some parties reporting regular interaction with Ministry of Justice officials and others having none at all. Smaller parties with fewer resources complained that the new regulation unfairly targeted them. According to political analysts, some parties believed that the Ministry of Justice's regulation was an attempt to sideline opposition parties, particularly prior to the 2014 presidential and provincial elections.

Participation of Women and Minorities: The constitution provides for seats for women and minorities in both houses of parliament. The constitution provides for at least 68 female delegates in the lower house of the national assembly, while 10 seats are provided for the Kuchi minority. According to the constitution, the president should appoint one-third of the members of the upper house, including two members with physical disabilities and two Kuchis. Fifty percent of the president's appointees to the upper house must be women. One seat in the upper house is reserved for the appointment of a Sikh or Hindu representative. On September 4, President Karzai issued a presidential decree reserving a seat in the lower house for a Sikh or Hindu in the next parliamentary elections in 2015. On December 15, the lower house voted to strike down the decree; final resolution was pending at year's end.

The legislatively mandated quota system provides for women to constitute more than 25 percent of the lower house of parliament. Exceeding the quota, women held 27 percent of seats in the lower house. Traditional societal practices sometimes continued to limit women's participation in politics and activities outside the home and community, including the need to have a male escort or permission to work, likely continued to influence the central government's male-dominated composition. The July Electoral Law reduced women's quotas on provincial councils from 25 percent to 20 percent and eliminated women's quotas entirely for district and village councils. Neither district nor village councils had yet been formed by year's end.

Women active in public life continued to face levels of threats and violence and were the targets of attacks by the Taliban and other insurgent groups. Most female parliamentarians reportedly experienced some kind of threat or intimidation, and many believed that the state could not or would not protect them. In August Fariba Kakar, a female member of parliament, was kidnapped at gunpoint in Ghazni and released in exchange for Taliban fighters one month later.

Female members of the High Peace Council continued to face impediments in participating in major decision making related to the peace process and were excluded from council delegations on some foreign visits. At year's end women filled eight of the 70 seats on the council.

There were three women in cabinet-level positions (Public Health, Social Affairs, and Women's Affairs).

The Pashtun ethnic group had more seats than any other ethnic group in both houses of parliament but did not have more than 50 percent of the seats. There was no evidence that specific societal groups were excluded. There were no laws preventing minorities from participating in political life, although different ethnic groups complained that they did not have equal access to local government jobs in provinces where they were a minority.

Section 4. Corruption and Lack of Transparency in Government

The law provides criminal penalties for official corruption. The government did not implement the law effectively, and there were reports that officials frequently engaged in corrupt practices with impunity. There were some reports of low-profile corruption cases successfully tried at the provincial level. The government made several commitments to combat corruption, including President Karzai's 2012 decree, but little progress had been made towards implementation at year's end. At the beginning of the year, the Attorney General's Office created a monitoring department, as required by the decree, and it began accepting referred cases. There was no progress on the cases reported as of year's end.

On June 30, a new law organizing the judiciary weakened the Control and Monitoring Department of the Supreme Court. The department had been considered effective in dealing with corruption within the judiciary in the districts and provinces. The new law eliminated the department's authority to conduct investigations, make arrests, and prosecute violators as well as some of its key positions.

Reports indicated corruption was endemic throughout society, and flows of money from the military, international donors, and the drug trade continued to exacerbate the problem. Reports indicated that many Afghans believed the government had not been effective in combating corruption. Corruption and uneven governance continued to play a significant role in allowing the Taliban to maintain its foothold in the east-central part of the country (the five provinces surrounding Kabul) and maintain influence in some parts of the southern provinces.

Prisoners and local NGOs reported that corruption was widespread across the justice system, particularly in connection with the prosecution of criminal cases and "buying" release from prison. There were also reports of money being paid to reduce prison sentences, halt an investigation, or have charges dismissed outright. The practice of criminalizing civil complaints was commonly used to settle business disputes or extort money from wealthy international investors.

During the year reports indicated a rise in incidents of "land grabbing" by both private and public actors. The most common type occurred when businesses illegally obtained property deeds from corrupt officials and sold the deeds to unsuspecting "homeowners," who would then get caught in criminal prosecutions. Other reports indicated that government officials grabbed land without compensation in order to swap the land for contracts or political favors.

Occasionally, provincial governments illegally confiscated land without due process or compensation to build public facilities.

Corruption: The case of Kabul Bank, which had been the country's largest private financial institution prior to its collapse in a huge bank fraud scandal that began unfolding in 2010, had not been resolved by year's end. Reportedly, nearly 50 billion Afghanis ($1 billion) of misappropriated funds were disbursed to politicians, ministers, and politically well-connected shareholders of the bank. By year's end less than 25 percent of the money had been recovered.

On March 5, the Kabul Bank Special Tribunal sentenced former chairman Sherkhan Farnood and former chief executive officer Khalilullah Ferozi to five years in prison for "breach of trust" and ordered them to make restitution. The Attorney General's Office indictment sent to the Special Tribunal in October 2012 also included the crimes of embezzlement and money laundering, both of which would allow for confiscation of the defendants' property. The conviction on breach of trust, however, did not allow authorities to confiscate assets or impose any penalties for failure to repay the funds. The attorney general appealed the verdict, and the case was pending at year's end.

The remaining 19 persons accused in the case, including minor bank officials and public officials, were convicted and sentenced to prison terms and fines that were generally considered disproportionately heavy in comparison with the sentences received by Farnood and Ferozi.

There were reports that the Attorney General's Office was unwilling or unable to pursue corrupt officials and that high-level officials who were arrested on corruption-related charges were released subsequent to political pressure. In addition there was anecdotal evidence that accusations of corruption on the part of others were used by corrupt officials to damage their opponents' reputations or to deflect attention from their own misdeeds. There were also reports that the Attorney General's Office compelled international contractors to settle claims made by Afghan subcontractors, regardless of the merits of the commercial disputes involved, and detained foreign employees of the contractors as leverage in the disputes (see section 1.d.).

Provincial police benefited financially from corruption at police checkpoints and from the narcotics industry. It was reported that ANP officers paid higher-level Ministry of Interior officials for their positions and to secure promotions. The justice system rarely pursued corruption cases, especially if they involved police, although authorities arrested and detained a provincial chief of police on drug trafficking charges. During the year the minister of interior also removed more than 40 police officers on charges of corruption, poor performance, and abuse of power, reportedly following a 10-month investigation.

In addition to official impunity issues, low salaries exacerbated government corruption. The international community worked with the national and provincial governance structures to address the problem of low salaries, but implementation of grade reform remained slow.

Credible sources reported that local police in many areas extorted a "tax" and inflicted violence at police checkpoints for nonpayment. Truck drivers complained that they had to pay bribes to security forces, insurgents, and bandits to allow their trucks to pass.

Police also reportedly extorted bribes from civilians in exchange for release from prison or to avoid arrest. Citizens also paid bribes to corrections and detention officials for the release of prisoners who had not been discharged at the end of their sentences.

The government made efforts to combat corruption within the security apparatus. Before the 2010 elections, the Ministry of Interior trained and deployed provincial inspectors general, who remained on duty after the elections. Their training continued. Merit-based promotion boards continued, with at least three candidates competing for each job; the process of instituting pay reform and electronic funds transfer for police salaries also continued.

The HOO oversees and develops the government's ability to mitigate corruption in line with commitments made at the 2010 London and 2012 Kabul conferences, and as directed by the 2012 presidential decree on good governance. Overall, the oversight office continued to be ineffective, with reports of corruption within the office itself.

Governors with reported involvement in the drug trade or records of human rights violations reportedly continued to receive executive appointments and served with relative impunity.

The media reported that the Afghanistan Chamber of Commerce and Industry established the first association for accountants and auditors in the country to improve transparency in financial systems and prevent corruption.

<u>Whistleblower Protection</u>: The penal code establishes protections for whistleblowers who report official corruption by making it a crime to either threaten or disclose the identity of the informant. In addition, the HOO law provides protection for whistleblowers who give information directly to the HOO. There was no evidence that these laws were being effectively implemented, however.

<u>Financial Disclosure</u>: The HOO must collect information from senior government officials on all sources and levels of personal income. The office must verify and publish the personal asset declarations of the most senior officials (those covered under article 154 of the constitution, plus provincial governors) on its internet website and in mass media that reach at least 40 percent of the public. While collection and publication occurred, there was only limited progress on the verification of such declarations by joint Afghan/international experts independent of the government. There is no legal penalty for any official who submits documentation with omissions or misrepresentations, undermining a key tool to identify possible wrongdoing. The government continued to make electronic direct deposits of police and military salaries and expanded a pilot project to pay police via mobile telephone in areas without banks, making salary payment a more transparent and accountable process and theoretically less subject to corruption.

<u>Public Access to Information</u>: The constitution provides citizens the right to access government information, except when access might violate the rights of others. Access to information from official sources continued to be limited due to a lack of clarity regarding citizens' right to access and a lack of transparency among government institutions. Civil society and media representatives sought passage of a law on freedom of access to information and worked with government officials to draft such laws.

Section 5. Governmental Attitude Regarding International and Nongovernmental Investigation of Alleged Violations of Human Rights

A wide variety of domestic and international human rights groups generally operated without government restriction, investigating and publishing their findings on human rights cases. While government officials were somewhat cooperative and responsive to their views, there were cases in which government officials intimidated human rights groups. Human rights activists continued to express concern that war criminals and human rights abusers remained in positions of power within the government. Powerful figures within the government blocked the release of the AIHRC report, *Conflict Mapping in Afghanistan since 1978*. As of year's end, the report had not been released.

The lack of security and instability in parts of the country continued to affect NGO activities. While insurgent groups and the Taliban directly targeted NGOs during the year, the domestic NGO Safety Office reported a 17 percent decrease in NGO security incidents in 2012, a trend that appeared to continue during the year.

Government Human Rights Bodies: The constitutionally mandated AIHRC continued to address human rights problems and operated with minimal government funding, relying almost exclusively on international donor funds. The mutual accountability framework agreed upon at the July 2012 Tokyo conference included provisions for expeditious enforcement of constitutional provisions and assurances that the AIHRC would be able to perform its appropriate functions. Nonetheless, President Karzai did not reappoint the AIHRC commissioners, whose terms had expired in 2011, until June. Civil society representatives asserted that several of the president's appointees were not independent, which allowed him to exercise greater control over independent democratic institutions, such as the AIHRC, and also questioned the new appointees' credibility and commitment to human rights.

Although President Karzai signed the Action Plan for Peace, Justice, and Reconciliation in 2006, the action plan had yet to be implemented, despite calls from civil society for transitional justice. The government's efforts focused primarily on reconciliation and negotiations with the Taliban led by the High Peace Council.

Three committees deal with human rights in the Wolesi Jirga (the lower house of parliament): the Gender, Civil Society, and Human Rights Committee; the Counternarcotics, Intoxicating Items, and Ethical Abuse Committee; and the Judicial, Administrative Reform, and Anticorruption Committee. In the Meshrano Jirga (the upper house of parliament), the Committee for Gender and Civil Society addresses human rights concerns.

Section 6. Discrimination, Societal Abuses, and Trafficking in Persons

While the constitution prohibits discrimination among citizens and provides for the equal rights of men and women, local customs and practices that discriminated against women prevailed in much of the country. The constitution does not explicitly address equal rights based on race, disability, language, or social status. There were reports of discrimination based on race, ethnicity, religion, and gender.

Women

Although the situation of women marginally improved during the year, domestic and international gender experts considered the country very dangerous for women, and women routinely expressed concern that social, political, and economic gains would be lost in the post-2014 transition.

Pursuant to the constitution, the 2009 Shia Personal Status Law governs family and marital issues for the approximately 19 percent of the population who are Shia. Although the law officially recognizes the Shia minority, the law does not adequately protect gender equality. Articles in the law of particular concern continued to be those on minimum age of marriage, polygyny, right of inheritance, right of self-determination, freedom of movement, sexual obligations, and guardianship.

Rape and Domestic Violence: The 2009 EVAW law, which was put into effect by presidential decree, criminalizes violence against women, including rape, battery, or beating; child and forced marriage; humiliation; intimidation; and the refusal of food. The law punishes rape with 16 to 20 years in prison. If the act results in the death of the victim, the law provides for the death sentence for the perpetrator. The law punishes the "violation of chastity of a woman…that does not result in adultery (such as touching)" with imprisonment of up to seven years. Under the law rape does not include spousal rape. The law was not widely understood, and some in the public and the religious communities deemed the law un-Islamic.

In May a female parliamentarian presented the law to parliament seeking additional reaffirmation of women's rights even although this was not technically necessary. This inadvertently led to the conservative male majority arguing against the law by saying the protections for women were un-Islamic. The speaker prevented the law from being overturned or amended and weakened by promptly ending debate and proposing that it be reviewed by a parliamentary committee, where it remained at year's end. The AIHRC, justice implementers, and civil society continued to make efforts to increase awareness of the law, despite the controversy. There was limited political will to implement the law, however, and authorities continued to fail to enforce it properly and successfully.

According to a survey by the Asia Foundation, fewer than one in five respondents said that an organization, institution, or authority existed in their area where women could go to have their problems resolved, while more than three-quarters said that there was no such organization in their area. Women who sought assistance under the EVAW law in case of rape often were subjected to virginity tests and in some instances had their cases converted into adultery cases. Interpretations of sharia also impeded successful prosecution of rape cases. Some female leaders believed that revisions and improvements to the EVAW law were needed, while others were primarily focused on implementation and enforcement.

As of August 1, there were 1,084 complaints registered with Violence against Women (VAW) prosecution units for crimes under the EVAW law, indicating a significant increase during the year compared with the approximately 1,500 cases registered in 2012. Provincial directorates of women's affairs and civil society activists indicated that this also reflected increased awareness of women's rights, which resulted in more complaints being reported. The vast majority of complaints brought under the EVAW law were resolved through family mediation. Government entities, such as the Ministry of Women's Affairs (MOWA) and law enforcement officials, referred a small number of cases, but civil society referred most of them.

Prosecutors and judges in some remote provinces were unaware of the EVAW law, and others were subject to community pressure to release defendants due to familial loyalties, threat of harm, or bribes. Reports indicated that men accused of rape often claimed the victim agreed to consensual sex, leading to adultery charges against the victim, or made false claims of marriage to the victim. The Ministry of Interior's Anticrime Police reported 397 cases of violence against women in 2012. The AIHRC and VAW unit reports indicated that registered incidents of violence against women continued to increase during the year. Statistics on convictions were unavailable by year's end. Rapes were difficult to document due to social stigma. Male victims seldom came forward due to fear of retribution or additional exploitation by authorities, but peer sexual abuse was common. Female victims faced stringent societal reprisal, from being deemed unfit for marriage to being imprisoned or a victim of extrajudicial killing.

In 2009, 16-year-old Gulnaz was raped by her cousin's husband and convicted and sentenced to a 12-year sentence for the crime of "adultery by force" because she refused to marry him. In December 2011 President Karzai pardoned Gulnaz following international criticism and lobbying by human rights groups after she served two-and-a-half years of her sentence. Gulnaz went to a women's shelter, where the law required her and her child to remain until she went to the home of a male family member. Her family refused to accept her, and in February, after 13 months in the shelter, Gulnaz bowed to social and family pressure and married her rapist.

In December 2011 police rescued a 15-year-old girl in Baghlan Province after they found her locked in a basement bathroom, having had her fingernails pulled out and being forced into prostitution by her 30-year-old husband and in-laws. The husband escaped arrest, but a court sentenced her mother-in-law and sister-in-law to 10 year's imprisonment in May 2012. In March the Supreme Court overturned the three convictions in the case, remanding the cases to the Kabul Appellate Court for reconsideration. The Kabul Appellate Court ordered that all three defendants be released from prison. The mother-in-law and father-in-law remained incarcerated while the Supreme Court reviewed that decision.

The penal code criminalizes assault, and courts entered judgments against domestic abusers under this provision. According to NGO reports, hundreds of thousands of women continued to suffer abuse at the hands of their husbands, fathers, brothers, armed individuals, parallel legal systems, and institutions of state, such as the police and justice systems. According to an AIHRC report on rape and honor killing, murders, assaults, and sexual violence against women commonly involved family members as suspects.

Police response to domestic violence was limited, in part due to low reporting, sympathetic attitudes toward perpetrators, and limited protection for victims. There were reports of government officials' complicity in violations of the EVAW law. The AIHRC reported that 14.6 percent of honor killings and sexual assaults were committed by police. In January a teenage girl seeking safe haven with a local Department of Women's Affairs allegedly was raped by six department guards while waiting to be transferred to a shelter. Some police and judicial officials were not aware or convinced that rape was a serious criminal offense, and investigating a rape case was generally not a priority. Even in instances when justice officials took rape seriously, some cases reportedly did not proceed due to bribery, family or tribal pressure, or other interference during the process. The AIHRC's report on rape and honor killing asserted that only 64 percent of cases referred to the justice sector were prosecuted or adjudicated correctly. The AIHRC and NGOs, however, confirmed that a majority of cases went unreported due to societal acceptance of the practice.

According to the AIHRC, between March and June there were more than 2,500 cases of violence against women reported. The AIHRC registered more than 280 women who had been killed by family members during 2011 and 2012 but asserted that most cases probably went unreported. The AIHRC also expressed concern that traditional and cultural violence, such as child and forced marriage, the practice of exchanging women to settle disputes (baadh), forced isolation, and honor killings, continued and appeared to be on the rise.

Most women did not seek legal assistance for domestic or sexual abuse because they did not know their rights or because they feared prosecution or return to their family or the perpetrator. Women sometimes turned to shelters for assistance and sometimes practiced self-immolation, and MOWA reported that cases of suicide as a result of domestic violence continued. NGOs that ran women's shelters in Kabul reported an increase in referrals from police, likely reflecting improved ANP training and awareness. Women's access to shelters also increased due to international efforts to open new shelters and expand to more remote provinces. Space at the 29 formal and informal shelters across the country, however, was insufficient. Women who could not be reunited with their families were compelled to remain in shelters indefinitely because "unaccompanied" women were not commonly accepted in society. The difficulty of finding durable solutions for women compelled to stay in shelters was compounded by societal attitudes toward shelters, the belief that "running away from home" is a serious violation of social mores, and the continued victimization of women who were raped but perceived by society as adulterers.

Women in need of shelter but who could not find it often ended up in prison, either due to a lack of shelter alternatives, for their own protection, or based on local interpretation of "running away" as a moral crime. Adultery, fornication, and kidnapping are crimes under the law. Women often were convicted of those crimes in situations of abuse, rape, or forced marriage, or on the basis of invalid evidence, including flawed virginity tests. Running away is not a crime under the law. As of September 30, 80.4 percent of female prisoners were incarcerated for moral crimes, according to GDPDC records. The records also indicated that the number of women incarcerated increased from 683 in May 2012 to 799 in May. The AIHRC and MOWA reported that approximately 25 percent of the female prison population had been incarcerated for either zina or "running away."

The Supreme Court acknowledged that women have a right to be free from violence in the home and indicated that women, who have left the home and approach relatives or government institutions for assistance with violence, have not committed a crime. There were reports that some justice officials conflated running away with the intent to commit adultery and proceeded with prosecution without regard to the conditions that prompted the woman to leave her home. In April 2012 the Attorney General's Office issued a circular to prosecutors stating that running away was not, on its own, a crime and should not be prosecuted. In May a Human Rights Watch report stated that convictions of women for running away had decreased since 2012.

In June the juvenile rehabilitation centers in Kabul, Gardez, Balkh, Nangarhar, Kunduz, and Herat admitted to ordering virginity tests to be conducted on all female detainees and prisoners. The tests, conducted at hospitals by the Ministry of Public Health, involved a gynecological examination to detect the presence of the hymen. The tests also often were ordered by the police, prosecutors, and courts and could be used as evidence of moral crimes if authorities desired.

In 2011 the government announced a plan to bring all shelters under MOWA's oversight. Human rights NGOs worked with MOWA to change the regulations and stop the proposed nationalization of shelters. The final shelter regulation authorizes MOWA to regulate all shelters but allows NGOs to continue to run them. In June 2012 the minister of justice equated shelters to brothels during a parliamentary conference on ending violence against women; he later apologized for the remarks. In May the parliamentary debate over the EVAW law reignited public debate over women's shelters. One member of parliament likened the shelters to brothels, and one prominent television channel began to broadcast antishelter programming daily. While MOWA, civil society, and the international community criticized the antishelter rhetoric, the existence and independent operation of shelters continued to be an issue under analysis.

There were reports that MOWA, as well as nongovernmental entities, sought to arrange marriages for women who could not return to their families.

Female police officers trained to help victims of domestic violence were hindered by instructions to wait for victims to reach out. There were 355 female response unit investigators nationwide working out of 146 offices, which were staffed primarily by female police officers who addressed violence and crimes against women, children, and families. Women serving in civilian and ANP positions in the Ministry of Interior offered mediation and resources to prevent future domestic violence.

<u>Harmful Traditional Practices</u>: The EVAW law criminalizes forced or underage marriage and baadh. According to the UN and Human Rights Watch, an estimated 70 percent of marriages were forced. Despite laws banning the practice, many brides continued to be younger than the legal marriage age of 16 (or 15 with a guardian's and a court's approval). A survey of married women between the ages of 20 and 24 found that 39 percent had been married before the age of 18. Very few marriages were registered, leaving forced marriages outside legal control. There were reports that women who sought assistance under the EVAW law in cases of forced marriage or rape were subjected to virginity tests.

Local officials occasionally imprisoned women at the request of family members for opposing the family's choice of a marriage partner or being charged with adultery or bigamy. There were also reports that local officials imprisoned women in place of a family member who had committed a crime but could not be located. Some women remained in detention facilities because they had run away from home to escape domestic violence or the prospect of forced marriage.

The AIHRC released its national inquiry on rape and honor killing report after a multi-year investigation. The commission reported that, between March 21, 2011, and April 21, 2013, there were 406 reported cases of honor killings and sexual assaults registered with the AIHRC. The unreported number was believed to be much higher and to include cases of suicide and self-immolation that covered honor killings. Under the penal code, a man convicted of honor killing after finding his wife committing adultery cannot be sentenced to more than two years' imprisonment.

There were reports of summary justice by the Taliban and other antigovernment elements resulting in extrajudicial executions. For example, a father executed his young daughter on April 22 in front of a crowd estimated at 300 persons in Badghis Province. Four religious scholars issued the execution order for alleged adultery and "running away." Later one of the scholars was arrested for ties to the Taliban, but at year's end the father and the other three scholars remained at large.

The wide range of violence against women also included trafficking and abduction.

<u>Sexual Harassment</u>: There is no law specifically prohibiting sexual harassment. In July the Ministry of Interior established a directive on sexual harassment, but it was not implemented. Women who walked outside alone or went to work often experienced abuse or harassment, including groping, or were followed on the streets in urban areas. Women who took on public roles that challenged gender

stereotypes (such as female lawmakers, political leaders, NGO leaders, police officers, and news broadcasters) continued to be intimidated by conservative elements or received death threats directed at them or their families. NGOs reported violence against women working in the public and nonprofit sectors, including killings, and initiated awareness-raising campaigns to mobilize groups against harassment. Female members of the ANP reported harassment by their male counterparts, and there were reports of intimidation of and discrimination against female ANP members and their families in their communities. According to Oxfam's September report, *Women and the Police*, the National Public Radio found allegations of widespread sexual abuse and rape of female police officers as well as evidence that senior police officers demanded sexual favors in exchange for promotions.

Reproductive Rights: Women generally exercised little decision-making authority regarding marriage, timing and number of pregnancies, birthing practices, and child education.

Couples were free from government discrimination, coercion, and violence to decide the number, spacing, and timing of their children, although family and community pressures to reproduce, the high prevalence of child and early marriages, and lack of accurate biological knowledge continued to limit their ability to do so. Women could expect to bear on average 5.1 children in their lifetimes. Oral contraceptives, intrauterine devices, injectable contraceptives, and condoms were available commercially and were provided at no cost in public health facilities and at subsidized rates in private health facilities and through community health workers. According to the 2012 *State of the World Population Report*, the maternal mortality rate in 2010 was 460 deaths per 100,000 live births. Although the situation improved, early marriage and pregnancy still put girls at greater risk for premature labor, complications during delivery, and death in childbirth. Postpartum hemorrhage and obstructed labor were key causes of maternal mortality. Only 34 percent of births were attended by a skilled health practitioner, and only 16 percent of girls and women between the ages of 15 and 49 used a modern form of contraception.

Discrimination: Women who reported cases of abuse or who sought legal redress for other matters reported discrimination within the judicial system. Some observers, including female judges, asserted that discrimination was a result of faulty implementation of law and cultural nuances, rather than the law itself. A woman's limited access to money and other resources to pay fines (or bribes) and the social requirement for women to have a male guardian affected women's access to and participation in the judicial system. Local practices were discriminatory against women in some areas, particularly in parts of the country where courts were not functional or knowledge of the law was minimal. Judges in some remote districts acknowledged wide influence by tribal authorities in preempting cases from the formal justice system. In the informal system, elders relied on interpretations of sharia and tribal customs, which generally discriminated against women. Many women reported limited access to justice in male-dominated tribal shuras, where proceedings focused on reconciliation with the community and family rather than the rights of the individual. Women in some villages were not allowed any access to dispute resolution mechanisms. Lack of awareness of their legal rights and illiteracy also limited women's ability to access justice. Women's advocacy groups reported that in some cases the government intervened informally with local courts to encourage them to interpret laws in ways favorable to women. Many cases in remote districts, however, were reportedly still resolved according to the local police officer's or prosecutor's discretion or interpretation of the law. When legal authorities were aware of the EVAW law and its implementation, women were in some cases able to get appropriate assistance. Prosecutors in some provinces, however, continued to be reluctant to use the EVAW law and brought no charges under the law, despite their awareness of its existence.

Police, prosecutors, and judges discriminated against women in criminal and civil legal proceedings stemming from violence and forced marriages. Enhanced availability of legal aid, including through female attorneys, provided some relief in formal justice system proceedings.

Cultural prohibitions on free travel and leaving the home unaccompanied prevented many women from working outside the home and reduced their access to education, health care, police protection, and other social services. In June clerics in Baghlan Province issued a religious edict (fatwa) with provisions limiting the rights of women – similar to those under the Taliban – which banned women from leaving home without a male relative, including when visiting medical clinics, and sought to shut down cosmetic shops. The Ulama Council issued statements that called for restrictions on women's ability to participate in society.

The law provides for equal work without discrimination, but there are no provisions for equal pay for equal work. Women faced discrimination in access to employment and terms of occupation. Some educated urban women found substantive work, but many were relegated to menial tasks. There were approximately 1,716 female police officers, constituting just 1.1 percent of the total police force. The government set having 5,000 female police officers by the end of the year as a goal but did not reach it. While the government made efforts to recruit additional female police officers, cultural mores and discrimination rendered recruitment and retention difficult.

The MOWA and NGOs continued to promote women's rights and freedoms. The Independent Administrative Reform and Civil Service Commission Gender Directorate did not successfully implement an action plan for increasing the percentage of women in the civil service to 30 percent by 2013. At year's end, there were at least 21 percent fewer women in the civil service than during 2012. According to the AIHRC, many women in the civil service could not meet the minimum qualification of a bachelor's degree imposed by the priority reform and restructuring system. MOWA, the primary government agency responsible for addressing gender policy and the needs of women, had offices in all provinces and established gender units in all ministries. Gender units were established at low ranks lacking major influence, and men typically dominated leadership positions. Although MOWA provincial offices assisted hundreds of women by providing legal and family counseling and referring women, they could not directly assist relevant organizations. The ministry and provincial line directorates continued to suffer from a lack of capacity and resources. Reports that MOWA provincial offices, such as in Ghor, returned abused women to their families continued.

The country achieved substantial improvements in health over the past decade, and public health statistics indicated a drop in maternal mortality. The overall health situation of women and children remained poor, however, particularly among nomadic and rural populations and those in insecure areas. Similar to males, female life expectancy was 64 years of age. Rural women continued to suffer disproportionately from insufficient numbers of skilled health personnel, particularly female health workers.

Compared to men, women and children were disproportionately victims of preventable deaths due to communicable diseases. Although free health services were provided in public facilities, many households could not afford certain costs related to medicines or transportation to health care facilities, and many women were not permitted to travel to health care facilities on their own.

Children

Birth Registration: Citizenship is transmitted by a citizen father to his child. Birth in the country or to a citizen mother alone is not sufficient. Adoption is not legally recognized.

Education: Education is mandatory up to the secondary level (six years for primary school and three years for lower secondary), and the law provides for free education up to and including the college level. Many children, however, did not attend school. According to the AIHRC, six million children worked instead of attending school.

In most regions boys and girls attended primary classes together but were separated for intermediate and secondary-level education. Of the country's 8.4 million children in school, the Ministry of Education estimated that 3.27 million, or 39 percent, were female. Many students, however, were not enrolled full time or dropped out early. A 2012 UNESCO report estimated that boys outnumbered girls by a ratio of two to one at the secondary level and four to one at the tertiary level.

The status of girls and women in education remained a matter of grave concern. Key obstacles to girls' education included poverty, early and forced marriage, insecurity, lack of family support, lack of female teachers, and the long distance to school. President Karzai's July 2012 Decree on Governance and Corruption addressed the lack of female teachers, particularly in conservative rural areas, by charging the Ministry of Education with recruiting an additional 11,000 teachers and increasing the number of district-level teacher training support centers to provide training opportunities for female teachers.

Violent attacks against schoolchildren, particularly girls, also hindered access to education. Violence impeded access to education in various sections of the country, particularly in areas controlled by the Taliban. The Taliban and other extremists threatened and attacked school officials, teachers, and students, particularly girls, and burned both boys' and girls' schools. While the Ministry of Education reported an increase in attacks on education employees during the year, neither the Ministry of Public Health, the Ministry of Education, nor the Ministry of Interior reported poisoning incidents during the year.

Insecurity, conservative attitudes, and poverty denied education to millions of school-age children, mainly in the southern and southeastern provinces. There were also reports of abduction and molestation. The lack of community-based, nearby schools was another factor inhibiting school attendance.

Child Abuse: NGOs reported increased numbers of child abuse victims during the year, and the problem remained endemic throughout the country. Such abuse included general neglect, physical abuse, sexual abuse, abandonment, and confined forced labor to pay off family debts. There were reports that police beat and sexually abused children, including a case in which a Baghlan provincial Ministry of Interior criminal investigative directorate commander was indicted after raping a 15-year-old girl. NGOs reported a predominantly punitive and retributive approach to juvenile justice throughout the country. Although it was against the law, corporal punishment in schools, rehabilitation centers, and other public institutions remained common.

Sexual abuse of children remained pervasive. On June 1, the AIHRC reported that sexual abuse of children had reached an all-time high. NGOs noted that girls were abused by extended family members, while boys were more frequently abused by men outside their families. NGOs noted that families often were complicit, allowing local strongmen to abuse their children in exchange for status or money. While the Ministry of Interior tracked cases of rape, most NGOs and observers estimated that the official numbers significantly underreported the phenomenon. The AIHRC reported an increase in rapes during the year, with most victims being children. Many child sexual abusers were not arrested, and there were reports that security officials and those connected to the ANP raped children with impunity. The practice of "bacha baazi" (dancing boys) – which involved powerful or wealthy local figures and businessmen sexually abusing young boys who were trained to dance in female clothes – was on the rise. Although the practice was believed to be more widespread in conservative rural areas, at least one media report alleged that it had become common in Kabul. Media reports also alleged that local authorities, including the police, were involved in the practice, but the government took few steps to discourage the abuse of boys or to prosecute or punish those involved.

Forced and Early Marriage: Despite a law setting the legal minimum age for marriage at 16 for girls and 18 for boys, international and local observers estimated that 60 percent of girls were married before the age of 16. During the EVAW law debate, conservative politicians publicly stated that it was un-Islamic to ban marriages of girls younger than 16. Under the EVAW law, those who arrange forced or underage marriages may be sentenced to imprisonment for not less than two years, but implementation of the law remained limited. The Law on Marriage states that marriage of a minor may be conducted with a guardian's consent.

By law a marriage contract requires verification that the bride is 16 years of age, but only a small fraction of the population had birth certificates. Following custom, some poor families pledged their daughters to marry in exchange for "bride money," although the practice was illegal. According to local NGOs, some girls as young as six or seven were promised in marriage, with the understanding that the actual marriage would be delayed until the child reached puberty. Reports indicated, however, that this delay was rarely observed and that young girls were sexually violated by the groom and by older men in the family, particularly if the groom was also a child. Media reports also noted the "opium bride" phenomenon, in which farmer families married off their daughters to settle debts to opium traffickers.

Sexual Exploitation of Children: Although pornography is a crime, child pornography is not specifically prohibited by law. Exploiting a child for sexual purposes, as was done with bacha baazi, also was widespread but not specified as a crime under the law.

Child Soldiers: See section 1.g.

Displaced Children: The Ministry of Labor, Social Affairs, Martyrs, and Disabled (MoLSAMD) and the AIHRC estimated the number of street children in the country at six million, but no new survey was undertaken by the National Census Directorate. Street children had little or no access to government services, although several NGOs provided access to basic needs, such as shelter and food.

Living conditions for children in orphanages were poor. The MoLSAMD oversaw 84 Child Protection Action Network centers and 70 residential orphanages, which were designed to provide vocational training to children from destitute families. Of these, 30 were privately funded orphanages and 40 were government-funded centers (but operated by NGOs by agreement with the ministry). NGOs reported that up to 80 percent of four- to 18-year-old children in the orphanages were not orphans but were children whose families could not provide food, shelter, or schooling. Children in orphanages reported mental, physical, and sexual abuse; sometimes were trafficked; and did not always have access to running water, winter heating, indoor plumbing, health services, recreational facilities, or education.

International Child Abductions: The country is not a party to the 1980 Hague Convention on the Civil Aspects of International Child Abduction.

Anti-Semitism

One Jew remained in the country at year's end. There were no reports of anti-Semitic acts.

Trafficking in Persons

See the Department of State's *Trafficking in Persons Report* at www.state.gov/j/tip/.

Persons with Disabilities

The constitution prohibits any kind of discrimination against citizens and requires the state to assist persons with disabilities and to protect their rights, including the rights to health care and financial protection. The constitution also requires the state to adopt measures to reintegrate and ensure the active participation in society of persons with disabilities. The 2010 Law on the Rights and Benefits of Disabled Persons provides for equal rights to, and the active participation of, such persons in society. MoLSAMD continued to implement a five-year national action plan through a memorandum of understanding with the Ministry of Information and Culture to implement public awareness programs on the rights of persons with disabilities through the national media as well as through a memorandum of understanding with the Ministry of Higher Education to provide scholarships for students with disabilities.

Updated and comprehensive data on persons with disabilities continued to be lacking. Handicap International carried out a National Disability Survey in 2005, which remained the most up-to-date source of information. The survey estimated that there were between 800,000 and 900,000 persons with disabilities in the country and that 20 percent of all households had at least one such person. MoLSAMD and NGOs, however, estimated that in 2013 there were two million persons with disabilities in the country, 61 percent of whom were women or children. Approximately 10 percent of persons with disabilities received financial support from the government.

Insecurity remained a challenge for disability programming. Insecurity in remote areas, where a disproportionate number of persons with disabilities lived, precluded delivery of assistance in some cases. The majority of buildings remained inaccessible to those with disabilities, prohibiting many from benefitting from education, health care, and other services.

Persons with disabilities faced challenges, such as limited access to educational opportunities; an inability to access government buildings, including Kabul International Airport; a lack of economic opportunities; and social exclusion. Persons with disabilities were mistreated in society and even by their own families as there was a common perception that persons had disabilities because they or their parents had "offended God."

In the Meshrano Jirga, two of the presidentially appointed seats were reserved for persons with disabilities.

National/Racial/Ethnic Minorities

Ethnic tensions between various groups continued to result in conflict and killings.

Societal discrimination against Shia Hazaras continued along class, race, and religious lines in the form of extortion of money through illegal taxation, forced recruitment and forced labor, physical abuse, and detention. Clashes between ethnic Hazaras and nomadic Kuchi tribes continued, with Hazaras alleging that Kuchis attempted to illegally seize their lands. In May Hazara students at Kabul University went on an eight-day hunger strike to protest alleged institutionalized ethnic discrimination and to call for the dismissal of some faculty members, including the dean. In July Rohullah Nekpa, the country's first and only Olympic medal winner, a two-time bronze medalist in tae kwon do, quit the sport to protest ethnic discrimination against Hazara athletes.

Sikhs and Hindus continued to face discrimination, reporting unequal access to government jobs and harassment in school, as well as verbal and physical abuse in public places. In July Sikh leaders reported that their shops, properties, and houses were taken by force and that they were attacked during religious ceremonies.

There were few reports of targeted discrimination against Ismailis (a minority Shia Muslim group).

Societal Abuses, Discrimination, and Acts of Violence Based on Sexual Orientation and Gender Identity

The law criminalizes consensual same-sex sexual conduct, and there were reports that harassment, violence, and detentions by police increased significantly during the year. NGOs reported that police arrested, robbed, and raped gay men. The law does not prohibit discrimination or harassment on the basis of sexual orientation or gender identity.

Homosexuality was widely seen as taboo and indecent. Members of the lesbian, gay, bisexual, and transgender (LGBT) community did not have access to health services and could be fired from their jobs because of their sexual orientation. Organizations devoted to protecting the freedom of LGBT persons remained underground because they could not be legally registered. Organizations carrying out health-related activities were able to provide services to gay men but not exclusively, due to fear of community reprisals. In one case authorities threatened a health organization's status as a registered NGO and cut off its access to medication until it proved that it did not provide services only to gay men.

Other Societal Violence or Discrimination

There were no confirmed reports of discrimination or violence against persons with HIV/AIDS, but there was reportedly serious societal stigma against persons with AIDS.

Section 7. Worker Rights

a. Freedom of Association and the Right to Collective Bargaining

The law provides for the right of workers to join and form independent unions and to conduct legal strikes and bargain collectively. The law, however, provides no definition of a union or its relationship with employers and members, nor does it establish a legal method for union registration. The law does not prohibit antiunion discrimination or provide for reinstatement of workers fired for union activity. Other than protecting the right to participate in a union, the law provides no other legal protection for union workers or workers seeking to unionize.

Although the law identifies the MoLSAMD Labor High Council as the highest decision-making body on labor-related issues, no implementing regulation to establish the council has been adopted. There was an inspection office within the ministry, but inspectors could only advise and make suggestions. As a result, labor law implementation remained limited because of a lack of central enforcement authority, implementing regulations that describe procedures and penalties for violations, funding, personnel, and political will.

The government allowed several unions to operate without interference or political influence. Freedom of association and the right to bargain collectively were generally respected, but most workers were not aware of these rights. This was particularly true of workers in rural areas or the agricultural sector, who had not formed unions. In urban areas the majority of workers participated in the informal sector as day laborers in construction, where there were neither unions nor collective bargaining.

b. Prohibition of Forced or Compulsory Labor

The constitution prohibits all forms of forced or compulsory labor. The law prescribes penalties, including a "maximum term" of imprisonment for forced labor (between eight and 15 years). Article 515 of the penal code also could be interpreted to criminalize a "foreign party's" coercive labor practices through fraud or deceit with a penalty of five to 15 years' imprisonment.

Government enforcement of the law was ineffective, and the government made minimal efforts to prevent and eliminate forced labor over the course of the year.

Forced labor occurred in practice. Men, women, and children were forced into poppy cultivation, domestic work, carpet weaving, brick kiln work, organized begging, and drug trafficking. NGO reports documented the practice of bonded labor, whereby customs allow families to force men, women, and children to work as a means to pay off debt or to settle grievances. The debt can continue from generation to generation, with children forced to work to pay off their parents' debt (see section 7.c.). Labor violations against migrant workers were common, especially the widespread practice of bonded labor in brick kiln facilities.

Also see the Department of State's *Trafficking in Persons Report* at www.state.gov/j/tip/.

c. Prohibition of Child Labor and Minimum Age for Employment

The labor law sets the minimum age for employment at 18 but permits 14 year olds to work as apprentices, allows children who are 15 and older to do "light work," and permits children who are 16 and 17to work up to 35 hours per week. Children under the age of 14 are prohibited from working under any circumstance. While the labor law prohibits the employment of children in work likely to threaten their health or cause disability, there is no list defining hazardous jobs.

The government lacked a specific policy on implementing the law's provisions on child labor. Generally poor institutional capacity was a serious impediment to effective enforcement of the labor law, and the government made minimal efforts during the year to prevent child labor or remove children from exploitative labor conditions. In addition, reports estimated that fewer than 10 percent of children had formal birth registrations, further limiting authorities' already weak capacity to enforce laws on the minimum age of employment.

Child labor remained a pervasive problem, with indications that the problem could become more widespread as families become more reliant on income produced by children as development aid drops and profit margins become lower. According to MoLSAMD estimates, nearly six million children worked in either the formal or informal sectors.

Child laborers worked as domestic servants, street vendors, peddlers, and shopkeepers, as well as in carpet weaving, brick making, the coal industry, and poppy harvesting. Children were also heavily employed in agriculture, mining (especially family-owned gem mines), commercial sexual exploitation (see section 6, children), transnational drug smuggling, and organized begging rings. Some sectors of child labor exposed children to land mines. Children faced numerous health and safety risks at work, and there were reports that children were exposed to sexual abuse by adult workers.

Also see the Department of Labor's *Findings on the Worst Forms of Child Labor* at www.dol.gov/ilab/programs/ocft/tda.htm.

d. Acceptable Conditions of Work

The minimum wage for government workers was 5,000 Afghanis ($100) per month. No specific minimum wage was set for the private sector, although the labor law states that it may not be less than the minimum wage of the government sector. According to the Central Statistics Office, 36 percent of the population earned wages below the poverty line of 1,250 Afghanis ($25) per month.

The law defines the standard workweek for both public sector and private sector employees as 40 hours: eight hours per day with one hour for lunch and noon prayers. The labor law makes no mention of day workers in the informal sector, leaving them completely unprotected. There are no occupational health and safety regulations or officially adopted standards. The law, however, provides for reduced standard workweeks for youths, pregnant women, nursing mothers, miners, and workers in other occupations that present health risks. The law provides workers with the right to receive wages, annual vacation time in addition to national holidays, compensation for injuries suffered in the line of work, overtime pay, health insurance for the employee and immediate family members, and other incidental allowances. The law prohibits compulsory work and stipulates that overtime work be subject to the agreement of the employee. The law prohibits women and minors (15 to 18 years of age) from engaging in physically challenging work, work that is harmful to health, and from working at night. The law also requires employers to provide daycare and nurseries for children.

The government did not effectively enforce these laws. MoLSAMD had only 20 inspectors for 34 provinces, and the inspectors had no legal authority to enter premises or impose sanctions for violations.

Employers often chose not to comply with the law or to hire workers informally. Most employees worked longer than 40 hours per week, were underpaid, and worked in poor conditions, particularly in the informal sector. Workers were generally unaware of the full extent of their labor rights under the law. Although comprehensive data on workplace accidents were unavailable, there were several reports of poor and dangerous working conditions. For example, in September at least 27 miners were killed in a collapse in a coal mine in the northern province of Samangan.